ISBN 978-1-331-43910-3
PIBN 10190350

English
Français
Deutsche
Italiano
Español
Português

www.forgottenbooks.com

Mythology Photography **Fiction**
Fishing Christianity **Art** Cooking
Essays Buddhism Freemasonry
Medicine **Biology** Music **Ancient
Egypt** Evolution Carpentry Physics
Dance Geology **Mathematics** Fitness
Shakespeare **Folklore** Yoga Marketing
Confidence Immortality Biographies
Poetry **Psychology** Witchcraft
Electronics Chemistry History **Law**
Accounting **Philosophy** Anthropology
Alchemy Drama Quantum Mechanics
Atheism Sexual Health **Ancient History**
Entrepreneurship Languages Sport
Paleontology Needlework Islam
Metaphysics Investment Archaeology
Parenting Statistics Criminology
Motivational

What Japan Says

about the

Anglo-Japanese Alliance

Compiled by

Kokusai News Agency

Price:

10 Sen, 5 Cents, 2 Pence

Published by

The Japan Times Publishing Co., Ltd.

1916

CONTENTS

340938

INTRODUCTION

In this booklet is reproduced a somewhat remarkable symposium presenting "the other side" or negative to the proposition advanced in the affirmative by a few doctrinnaires and eagerly seized upon by the German agents or echoed by those whom Baron Kato—in his speech at Osaka—classed as "certain week-kneed' Jaanese." Their suggestion was that Japan is opposed to the Anglo-Japanese Alliance and seeks to find excuse for breaking ot. The negative is overwhelming. From representative men of every class and every affiliation somes a denial. The German newspapers and the mischievous newspaper correspondents in Berlin and Tokyo take the affirmative. But, through the columns of the "THE JAPAN TIMES," it must have been demonstrated to the meanest intelligence that there is no foundation for the assertion, except as may be found in the essays of a few academic writers, sophomeric controversialists and a number of worthy people who may be depended upon to "pick the wrong horse" anyhow.

The series of Special interviews printed here give the opinions of

Count Okuma, Premier of Japan.

Baron Takahashi, Former President of the Bank of Japan and one of the strong Opposition Members of the Upper House.

Baron Ishii, Minister for Foreign Affairs.

Mr. B. Nakano, President of the Tokyo Chamber of Commerce.

Mr. S. Shimada, Speaker of the House of Representatives.

Mr. T. Tokonami, Member of Parliament. Prominent leader of the Opposition in the Lower House.

Hon. K. Minoura, Minister of Communications and veteran Chief of the "Hochi."

Mr. K. Ishikawa, Chief Editor of the "Jiji"—powerful independent newspaper.

Doctor J. Soyeda, President of the Government Railway Board and Economic Expert.

Baron Shibusawa, Leader and "Doyen" of the Financial and Commercial Army of Japan.

General Count Terauchi, Governor-General of Chosen; former Minister of War and active virile administrator.

Baron Sakatani, Former Minister of Finance and Government Delegate to Economic Conference in Paris.

Baron Kato, Former Minister for Foreign Affairs; Leader of the Doshi-kai. and powerful representative of modern Japan.

Mr. C. Matsuyama, Editor-in-Chief of the "Asahi," one of the great newspapers of the Far East.

Baron Megata, One of the leaders of the Opposition in the Upper House; Economic Expert, and formerly in charge of Korean finances.

Mr. M. Naruse, Vice-President of the Fifteenth Bank, President of The Teiyu Bank, and representative of Younger Japan.

Mr. Y. Ozaki, Minister of Justice and political leader in the House of Representatives.

Mr. N. Uyeshima, Editor-in-Chief for twenty years of the "Hochi," the great popular newspaper of Japan.

Mr. S. Hayakawa, Director of the great Mitsui interests and a leading financier.

Mr. E. Kamada, President of Keio University, and prominent educator. and author.

Mr. J. Inouye, President of the Yokohama Specie Bank, the most powerful active banking institution in the Far East.

These gentlemen have been frank in the expression of their views. A careful summarizing would give results as follows:

1.—The Anglo-Japanese Alliance is regarded in Japan by all leaders of public opinion and thought as a vital necessity.

2.—With changed conditions after the war, some clauses and terms of the present treaty must be altered so as to bring the alliance into harmony with the situation and the responsibilities of Great Britain and Japan.

3.—The controversy in a section of the press is largely "local politics," or an effort to create some dissatisfaction with the present Cabinet.

4.—The policy of Japan with regard to Great Britain is a fixed policy and no change of Cabinet can change that policy.

5.—Any discussion of the Alliance at this time is deprecated throughout this country and any criticism of England or of the Allies is regarded with distinct disfavour as unchivalrous and un-Japanese.

6.—While, unquestionably, this is the position of a vast majority of the people of this country of all classes, it is, nevertheless, a fact that an element of the people of Japan have begun to regard the British in the Far East with suspicion and disfavour. This feeling and this element has been fostered and catered to by sensational newspapers and by the enemy agent in Japan.

7.—The attitude of British resident in the Far East towards the Japanese has given cause for Japanese antagonism and bitterness. The representative Japanese interviewed have drawn attention to this in the hope that a realization of the cause may abate the feeling on both sides; that a more wholesome sense of fairness and of justice may bring about a mutual recognition of real character, and thus serve to place both on their guard against a mischievous common enemy.

8.—The agitation in the press is not approved or participated in by the larger newspapers, but it has served a purpose in providing the enemies of Japan and the enemies of Great Britain with a means of creating suspicion of the sincerity and honesty of Japan and at the same time casting doubt upon the friendship of Great Britain, or the freedom from race prejudice on both sides. The agitation in a few newspapers; the publication and wide-spread circulation of the translations of the newspaper comment and writings of newspaper contributors have afforded a great opportunity to those whose object it is to create and enlarge a breach between Japan and Great Britain and between Japan and America. But, at least, the expressions of opinion by the leading men of all parties and opinion in Japan has given "the other side." Up to the time this was started, the one side had it all to themselves and the cry of the mischief-maker was that the leading men, officials, and publicists of Japan were openly expressing antagonism to the Alliance and criticism of England, and that no one said anything on the other side. This cannot be said again with truth. In fact, it was never true that the leading men or officials of Japan were taking sides against their ally.

In the course of this series of interviews, it has been made abundantly clear that Japan and the Japanese stand by the Alliance and loyally by their ally in the present struggle.

Almost with the outbreak of the war a year and a half ago, the Germans began their campaign. At first, the Japanese Government, with an overweening confidence and an over-done courtesy, permitted these to "buy with them, sell with them, walk with them, talk with them and so forth" as, indeed, with almost equal over-indulgence and dangerous courtesy they are permitted to trade to-day. But the danger is too evident to be ignored and any tradal advantage to a few individuals is much more than cancelled by the inimical activities of all those who at this time are seeking to create dissension between all or any of those allied in strangling the "forces of evil."

It must not be thought for a moment that these interviews are taken haphazard

6

nor do they exhaust the opinions available. On the contrary hundreds of representative men will readily talk but these adequately voice the opinion of Japan.

Premier Count Okuma.

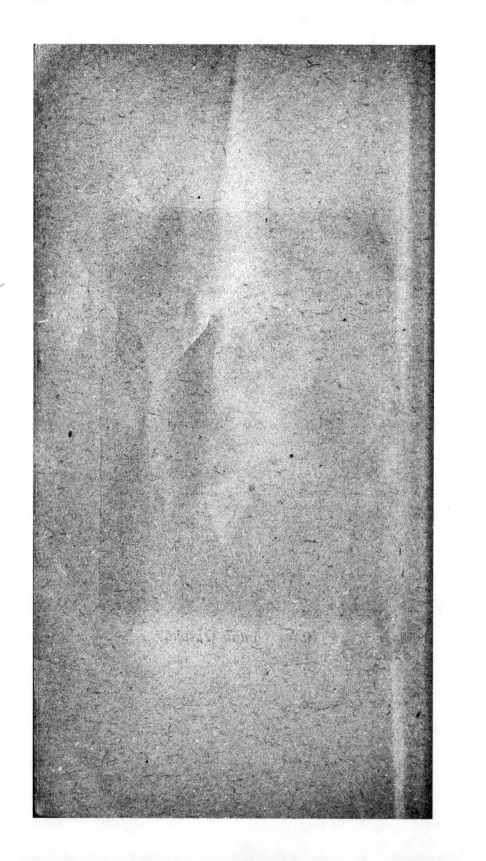

COUNT OKUMA IS EMPHATIC

The Premier of Japan Speaks with Characteristic Freedom and Frankness on the Subject of the Relations Between Great Britain and Japan— Present and Future

"We must stick together—we friends and allies—Japan and Great Britain, France and Russia—all, in order that we may crush Germany, our common enemy."

This was the answer of Count Okuma, the Premier, when asked if he would express his views on the agitation in a minor section of the Japanese press on the subject of the Anglo-Japanese Alliance and the criticisms which are represented abroad as constituting ground for the belief that Japan is not so friendly to England as had been generally thought.

"Any allegation that Japan is insincere in her friendship for or disloyal to her treaty with Great Britain is utterly false," he went on.

"The spirit of chivalry and loyalty to a friend is strong among the Japanese and this spirit has been manifested in

11

many ways since the outbreak of the war. I have no fear that the leading men of America, or of any other country will doubt Japan's sincerity or loyalty because of the writings and mouthings of a sensational newspaper any more than we of Japan doubt the friendship or the loyalty of England or America because a few newspapers say unkind things or publish untruths about us.

"We are doing everything we can to assist England in fighting her enemy.

"It is true that recently a small section of the Japanese press has taken a stand that might be regarded as anti-British. It has been suggested to me that such newspapers should be rigorously dealt with; but I regard the muzzling of the press as a dangerous thing to do unless the newspapers overstep the bounds. The absolute freedom of the press is a principle to which I have always adhered; besides, everyone should endeavour to take a broad view of any situation and if we do so in this case it will readily be seen that a so-called anti-British sentiment is confined to an extremely limited circle and that, indeed, the vast majority of the people of this country and of the press of Japan is extremely friendly to England and the allies.

"There are dissentients in all countries. They are to be found principally in local politics and these make international affairs a weapon with which to attack the Government.

"Just as a few Japanese newspapers say unfriendly things about Great Britain, we find some of the English or American newspapers saying unfriendly things about Japan. But we do not regard such irresponsible and petty utterances as representing the sentiment of a majority.

"I assert positively, without any fear of successful contradiction, that Japan is loyal to her alliance, friendly to Great Britain and faithful to all her undertakings. The Anglo-Japanese Alliance is just as strong to-day as ever it was. Japan benefits by the alliance and so does Great Britain.

"For the present we must relegate petty bickerings and narrow considerations to the background of national and international affairs.

"We must stick together—Great Britain and Japan, Russia and France, Italy and all others, in order that we may crush Germany—our common foe."

Minister of Foreign Affairs, Baron Ishii.

MINISTER FOR FOREIGN AFFAIRS

Baron Ishii Says There Should be no Ebb from One Gentleman to Another—Reassert His Good Faith or Give Again His Pledges to a Friend

Baron Ishii, Minister for Foreign Affairs, speaks ex cathedra—from a close and very intimate knowledge of the conduct of foreign affairs in this country, as well as a sympathetic and very human touch with the "man in the street."

Baron Ishii has for very many years been identified with the work of Japan's Foreign Office. He served as Chief of Bureaux and as Vice-Minister holding the latter position for some years under the late Marquis Komura, who is now conceded to have been one of the most brilliant and forceful foreign ministers Japan has had. Up to a few months ago, Baron Ishii was Ambassador to France and was called back to succeed Baron Kato.

Baron Ishii was asked to express an opinion as to the relations between Great Britain and Japan as affected by the recent agitation in the opposition newspapers. He said:

17

"No thoughtful or sensible person can doubt the sincerity of Japan in the position she has taken as to the present world struggle. The record speaks for itself and I would consider it undignified and superfluous now to make protestation or re-assertions of Japan's loyalty. The real Japan resents the bare insinuation of disloyalty and particularly of disloyalty to a friend in trouble.

"In normal times, with a world at peace, arguments and discussions over the terms and conditions of existing international treaties are permissible; indeed, they are desirable. But now, with the world at war, with our friend and ally engaging a relentless enemy, is not the time for such discussion or for dissension. We realize the obligation that lies upon us in the form of a treaty of alliance, but I may say that Japan is bound to England not by the ties of a treaty of alliance but by the closer bonds of mutual friendship and of mutual gratitude.

"The Frenchman has an expression which fits the case—Noblesse oblige—and so it will be with Japan while this war lasts and afterward.

"Local and national political explosives sometimes invade international territory. They appear formidable and are really harmless, but are taken seriously by the

"In spite of the efforts of our common enemy to sow the seeds of discord, I believe this war is going to bring the world closer together in mutual understanding and when that time of fuller understanding has been reached, there will be no call from the gentlemen of other countries to the gentlemen of Japan to reassert their pledges or protest their good faith."

Count Terauchi, Soldier and Diplomat.

GENERAL COUNT TERAUCHI
ON FRIENDSHIP

General Count Terauchi, soldier, diplomat and statesman, former Minister of
War and present Governor General of
Chosen (Korea) is beyond question one
of the most virile and effective administra-
tors and leaders in public life in the consideration of the public in Japan, and
perhaps abroad. Few living among the
men of achievement in the records of the
history of the world's development in the
last twenty years have played a larger
part than Count Terauchi.

"It is not surprising to me," writes
Count Terauchi, "that a sinister movement
is on foot to disturb relations between
Great Britain and Japan.

"There have existed in all ages makers
of mischief between friendly nations."

Count Terauchi, in the very prime of
matured manhood, has spent a life of ex-
traordinary activity and usefulness since
1871, when at nineteen years of age he
was appointed second lieutenant. He was
educated at a military school in France
a d reached the rank of Major-General in

1894. In the interim, he was three years attaché to the Legation in Paris, secretary to the Minister for War and Director of the Military Academy.

Count **Terauchi** took part in the Saigo rebellion, and, in the war with China, was supervisor of transport. But his first great prominence and administrative triumph was achieved during the war with Russia when, as War Minister, his splendid abilities as an administrator won the admiration of everyone who knows the history of that campaign.

Laying down the Portfolio in 1910, Count Terauchi became the Viceroy and Governor General of Chosen (Korea), and it has been in this great work of the rehabilitation of a country and a people that he has won his highest place in history, higher, indeed, than any he may hereafter win. Count Terauchi has now been the head of affairs on the Peninsula for six years but in that time has accomplished more for the country than can be accorded to any colonial administrator for any country in a similar period. He is a martinet as a disciplinarian, a careful economist, but just, generous and—even his worst enemies and severest critics admit —an honest man. Count Terauchi has more than once been approached to organize a cabinet as Premier of Japan and possibly one day may accept the task. But, wherever he may go, his greatest work will have been in the land which he found in squalor and in gloom, but where now prosperity and hope make life for its people worth living.

On the subject of the effort to create an impression abroad that Japan is not loyal to England, Count Terauchi said:

"In my opinion, it is not surprising at all that such a sinister movement is on foot, but if a friendship is to be shaken by any intrigue then the friendship is not firm enough to be real and lasting.

"The Alliance between Japan and Great Britain, closely cemented as it is, can in no wise be affected by press agitation.

"There can be no doubt that men of intelligence and character in both countries will adhere to and support this alliance with sincerity, and in neither country will there be the least question or misgiving as to the real object of the alliance or that it is of great mutual benefit. Already the object and the mutual benefit have been amply demonstrated.

"I most firmly believe that the relations between Japan and Great Britain are too amicable, and stand upon too firm a footing, to be shaken by the reprehensible methods of publicists and writers of questionable character and standing of either country."

H. E. Baron Kato.

BARON KATO ON THE GREAT
ALLIANCE

Baron Kato, four times Minister for Foreign Affairs, Ambassador to the Court of St. James, and the present leader of the Doshi-kai—the controlling influence of the House of Representatives, is the younger of the men who must be regarded as directing the course of Japan at the present time. Like all men of character, outspoken zeal and staunch loyalty to a friend as to a principle, Baron Kato has enemies and is reported by them to be unpopular. But he is known as a man of courage, frank to a degree and his political opponents respect him. Baron Kato was asked to depart from his customary reserve in dealing with the press and to give his views on the agitation started by a small element of the Japanese opposition and newspapers—an agitation that has been fostered and spread abroad until the public has commenced to believe that, after all, perhaps Japan might be considering a change of policy and a transference of her friendship.

Baron Kato was not disinclined to speak, but pointed out that his own position in the matter was well known—referring more particularly to a most interesting and exhaustive review of Japan's attitude towards Great Britain and the Alliance, given by him to the "Mainichi" of Osaka and published on January 1, 1915. Baron Kato said:

"It matters not who takes the reins of Government in this country or what cabinet is in power, our attitude towards England and the Alliance will remain the same. The people of Japan want the alliance and will want to continue this treaty of friendship and of mutual defense for all time to come. It is the rock on which our foreign policies stand. All other ententes and agreements are merely supplementary to this main plank in our national platform. No ministerial change can alter this position or this policy.

"The Anglo-Japanese Alliance stands for the peace of and peace in the Far East. If any man thinks this Alliance was conceived or entered into simply because it might be useful in times of war, he is mistaken.

"In its relation to the situation in China, for instance, the Alliance is one of peaceful guardianship, safeguarding China's integrity and the principle of equal opportunity which are as essential in conserving the interests of Japan as those of Great Britain.

"So long as the Anglo-Japanese Alliance stands, no power can break the integrity of China or really threaten the principle of equal opportunity. If Japan alone were to attempt this it would have to mean a tremendously increased outlay upon army and navy.

"The Anglo-Japanese Alliance has vastly increased the prestige of Japan. The moral effect has been and is incalculable England is our friend and England is always loyal to her friends. This all other powers know and have known. No country can go to war with us without having first to reckon with Great Britain. We cannot compute in figures what this Alliance has been worth to Japan.

"But the Anglo-Japanese Alliance is beneficial to Great Britain also. During the present war, Great Britain has been able to withdraw her ships from the Far East, whereas, if the Alliance had not been active and as actively carried out by Japan, a considerable portion of the British fleet must have been sent to these waters.

"It is true that in both countries publicists have objected to the Alliance for racial, religious, or commercial reasons. Some contend that Great Britain is hampered in her activities by the Alliance; but these protests do not disturb the British authorities or affect the intellectual people of England.

"In Japan, too, there has been a dissen-

31

.tient voice, but the government of the day —-whatever it may be, and those who understand the relations between Great Britain and Japan are no more disturbed. by this and no less appreciative of the value and benefit of the alliance than the same classes in Great Britain.

"It is only those who do not know the history of the Alliance and those who do not comprehend its real object who indulge in far-fetched and foolish criticisms.

"Even between relatives and families, sacrifices must be made on both sides if its smoothness is to be secured and maintained. No alliance or agreement can be made the instrument for benefit of one party alone. It is, therefore, in the mutual benefits derived that the permanency of the Alliance remains and friendly co-operation and relations secured."

Baron Makino, Privy Councillor,
Ex-Minister of Foreign Affairs.

BARON MAKINO

Baron Makino, Privy Councillor, beyond doubt speaks for the best there is in Japan. He was formerly Minister for Foreign Affairs, Minister of Education, Minister to Rome, Ambassador to Vienna and has been closely identified with every international movement in this country. When called upon, he readily responded to the request for a statement as to the Anglo-Japanese alliance and the agitation recently conducted by a few newspapers and writers.

Baron Makino said:

"During the past quarter of a century the great nations of the world have consummated many important international alliances and ententes. These have now been called into active operation to an extent which even their wisest negotiators and signatories did not anticipate. But the making of these treaties has now proved to have been vital."

"If we review the history of these alliances and ententes, the Russo-French Alliance, the Anglo-French Entente and the Triple Alliance, we must readily realize that all sorts of criticisms were

directed against the treaties and their
makers. Those strictures, though sometimes forceful, did not disturb or alter
the fundamentals of any of the great
pacts.

"The Anglo-Japanese Alliance has been
favourably received ever since its inau-
guration. Few treaties written into the
pages of diplomatic history were complet-
ed with greater smoothness. Criticisms
naturally there have been on both sides,
but they have made no difference. This
alliance has been most beneficial to the
contracting parties, both in times of peace
and in this present war. The peoples of
Great Britain and Japan are fully aware
of this fact."

"I regret to see, however, that of late,
in this country a few publicists and writers appear to have become seized with
an altogether erroneous conception of
the real purposes and the real value of
the alliance. Their criticisms, as I read
them, are based upon relations in China
of Englishmen and Japanese. But if we
look into the troubled waters a little
deeper, we must soon find that these critics have only seen things that appear on
the surface. They have failed to give
due weight and consideration to important
things that underlie the lighter and more
trivial. In my opinion, these dissentients
do not, by any means, constitute a lever
that can ever shift the cornerstones of
the Anglo-Japanese Alliance."

"The well informed on diplomatic affairs of this and other countries do not, by an overwhelming majority, fail to give ample recognition of the important part the Alliance has played in preventing the Far East from becoming much more deeply involved as a theatre of war."

"There are some, I believe, who assert that the value of the Alliance will largely be lost after the present war. This is thoughtless; it is, in fact, a dangerous contention. I firmly believe that after the war this Alliance will become increasingly effective and active, because the Chinese situation will remain a serious problem in the Far East, and the Anglo-Japanese Alliance, which strongly upholds the peace of the Far East and the integrity of China, will be certainly a controlling factor in the shaping of destiny in the Orient. Moreover, Great Britain is a great sea power, so also in a lesser degree, is Japan, and the waters of this globe unite these two friendly nations everywhere. The co-operation, therefore, of these two powerful maritime empires will be a most effective factor in keeping the peace of the world, as they have been effective factors during the present war."

"Those who fail to appreciate the full value of the Anglo-Japanese Alliance might test their position by placing themselves, for the moment, in the position of not having this Alliance. They will then have a better perspective. The removal of this great guarantee would at once reveal a menace and a source of great anxiety.''

"I must again assert, without any fear of effective contradiction, that the criticisms we have seen do not injure the foundation of the existing Alliance. Moreover, I emphatically believe that after the war, this great alliance will be the main stronghold of Japanese diplomacy. There may be found some minor clauses that require alteration to bring the whole into harmony with changed conditions, but no minor change in verbiage will affect the main body of this splendidly conceived and loyally supported alliance.''

"I wish to emphasize the necessity for, and the great usefulness of, the Anglo-Japanese Alliance in the advancement of civilization; the final maintenance of honourable and beneficent peace and the security of nations."

Baron Shibusawa.

OFFENSIVE AND FALSE

Baron Shibusawa the Doyen of Japan's Commercial Men Gives His Views on the Subject and Condemns those Who Belittle Value of Alliance

"I am quite sure that if and when any revision of the Anglo-Japanese Alliance may be found to be necessary in order to bring it into conformity with changed conditions, the revision may be left in the hands of the authorities of both countries with perfect safety to all concerned, and that it will be properly and satisfactorily attended to when suitable opportunity offers. But the present is not the time to make changes or to bring on discussions, Now is the time to live up to all our undertakings and to demonstrate the moral tone of this nation."

A careful reading of this enunciation by Baron Shibusawa will bring satisfaction to all concerned. There is nothing cryptic; there is no double meaning. The point is that the man who is known everywhere as the doyen of the Corps Commerciale in Japan; the wise, sound and seasoned leader of finance, of commerce, and of great philanthropic undertakings in this country, finds nothing in the Alliance at which to cavil, but even if he did, he says this is no time for Japan to seek a change.

"An obligation must be fulfilled. An agreement or a promise can in no way be evaded by a nation or by an individual. Japan is not seeking a change and is only endeavoring to find a way to help, not to hinder her ally."

The name of Baron Shibusawa calls for no special heralding or eulogy. Certain it is that at seventy-six years of age he is "The Grand Old Man" of the Japanese commercial world, occupying the same position in his own sphere that Count Okuma holds in the political world to-day.

Baron Shibusawa's first visit to the West was when he went to Europe in the year 1867, and since that time, even up to 1916, he has made occasional visits to America or Europe, in order to keep in touch with men, manners and affairs.

No man in Japan represents more, or can command a more respectful hearing, than Baron Shibusawa. It may safely be said that he represents the commercial element and that when he speaks he commands not only a hearing, but an overwhelming following and support.

France and of Russia—owe much. He has stood as the supporter of international good relations and good understanding for the

One thing may be said with safety, that to Baron Shibusawa—the commercial men of the West—of England and America, of last half century. He has stood for what is highest in the commercial life of all countries,—integrity, and "a square deal." Baron Shibusawa spoke on the subject of the recent attempt to create a division between Japan and Great Britain with even more than customary and characteristic vehemence. He said:

"The suggestion that Japan might consider a change in the Alliance at this time is not only a suggestion of what is false, but it is particularly offensive to the element I represent in Japan, as indeed it is offensive to all self-respecting people of this country.

"Even if Japan had no further need for assistance from England," he said, "there would be no question of a 'cooling off' or of the making of friends with her enemies. We do not desert a friend because we have nothing further to gain from him. We are not mercenaries.

"Nations, like individuals, must be guided by moral principles. Whether there were need for the Anglo-Japanese Alliance or not, we must remain true and loyal in every sense to a friend in trouble.

"We should keep on looking back, as well as forward. England was our friend when we were working our up-hill way and when we stood most in need of a friend. We do not forget.

"Even if our publicists should be able to convince us that there is no need for the Anglo-Japanese Alliance—and I think it will take a long time to bring us to this conviction—we would still remain loyal to our friendship and its obligations. A selfish and a self-seeking mercenary is intolerable in the case of a nation as in the case of a man or a woman. We are too proud of our traditions to allow any mercenary to mislead or to misrepresent us. We would sacrifice almost everything except honour—we would lose everything and bring ourselves to the close boundary of bankruptcy in the support of a friend and an ally.

"Some people say that there is no morality between nations. I do not agree with this. If morality did not guide nations in their dealings one with the other, this world would be a miserable place to live in. There could be no assurance of peace on earth, and it is for the assurance of such a peace that Japan and Great Britain stand together and will so stand shoulder to shoulder while this war lasts.

44

"It was because Germany would not observe her moral obligations in her international dealings that this war was brought on the world, and the Allies are now fighting to force Germany to the observance of an international code.

"I am no statesman and I am content to leave the wording of treaties and engagements to the statesmen of the countries making them, because they are patriotic and honest men, irrespective of party or of politics. Above all things, I desire to impress upon the public that this is no time for carpings, criticisms or dissensions. Let us safeguard Japan's prestige for international morality."

BARON TAKAHASHI

Active and Virile Representative of the Opposition Says No Cabinet will Change Attitude of Japan

Perhaps none of the men in touch with current events in Japan and abroad can speak with higher authority or as representing more capably the opinions of those who know public sentiment in Japan than Baron Takahashi, leading member of the Opposition in the House of Peers and former Minister of Finance, Governor of the Bank of Japan and President of the Yokohama Specie Bank.

Baron Takahashi may be regarded as one of the leading, virile men of Japan, who, closely in touch with events for the last twenty years, speaks as one unhampered by official surroundings. Baron Takahashi's views on the subject of the agitation against the Anglo-Japanese Alliance are particularly interesting, because, as is well known, he has been one of the most stalwart opponents of the present Government's foreign policies. When asked to give his views, Baron Takahashi said:

"The leading men of this country—the men of all classes, occupations or political leanings are in sympathy with Great Britain and the Allies. A consensus of the well-balanced opinion of the Empire will show the whole people to be in perfect accord as upholding the Anglo-Japanese Alliance. This is true in political, social, educational and economic circles. There is, in fact, no real division of opinion.

"I can see how difficult it is for foreigners to understand why the press agitation on the subject of the Alliance was commenced and kept up for some time. It must be borne in mind that the competence of the present Government to deal with foreign policies and diplomatic affairs has been seriously questioned by the Opposition. Hence, the Opposition press has sought to embarrass the majority during this session of the Diet and to draw sympathy by appeals to prejudice. The Opposition press and, indeed, many of the members of the Opposition have gone so far as to openly assert that Baron Kato, the former Minister for Foreign Affairs and the leader of the Government supporters in the last Diet is completely under the thumb of Great Britain—"Private Secretary to Sir Edward Grey," as one speaker said. Now, if this is said in the Diet, and the dependence of Baron Kato upon British influence is popularly believed, it gives the press a peg on which to base attack. Hence, in this acute state of public opinion, it is not difficult to understand how an opportunist cry may secure a vogue for a short time.

"I am a member of the Opposition. I doubt the competence and the ability of the present ministry and believe the country could do better, but the loyalty of Japan to Great Britain and the Anglo-Japanese Alliance is as fixed as any great principle of the nation and the agitation need not cause our friends a moment's uneasiness.

"Friendship for Great Britain, France, America, and the allied countries is not a policy inaugurated by this Cabinet and the fall of the Cabinet would not change the foreign policy of the Government by one hair's breadth."

Mr. Buei Nakano, President of Tokyo.
Chamber of Commerce

PRESIDENT NAKANO'S VIEWS

"Among the business men of Japan, to my knowledge, no one shares or approves the agitation started by the "Yamato Shimbun" and supported by a very few irresponsible newspapers."

Mr. Buei Nakano, President of the Tokyo Chamber of Commerce used these words as an emphatic preamble. Mr. Nakano may be regarded as, above all others, the one business man in Japan most closely in touch with all sorts and conditions of business men For many years, he has occupied his present position. He holds the respect, confidence, and high esteem of the business men of this country and, in fact, of the commercial world outside. Of the best Samurai ancestors, he entered upon an active business and administrative career in the year 1872 and, in the year 1881, was a secretary of the Department of Agriculture and Commerce. Since that time, he has been closely identified with the active political, commercial and administrative life of Japan. He has been elected a member of Parliament eight times in succession, and is at present also Chairman of the Tokyo City Assembly.

Mr. Nakano was quite ready to speak frankly on the subject of the Anglo-Japanese relations and to give his views on the press agitation in connection with a suggested change in the Alliance.

"Personally," said Mr. Nakano, "I am at a loss to understand what spirit prompts this harmful and unseemly discussion. I can see no ground for criticism or for complaint; nor, indeed, can I understand why any section of the foreign press or public should attach the slightest importance or significance to this petty press agitation. We business men of Japan usually disregard trivial and worthless arguments and discussions in the newspapers. The present agitation, the criticisms and the talk of the minor press do not represent the opinion of a majority of our people, or, indeed, of any part of the nation, to whose opinion importance may be placed. The foreign public, however, may have gained an entirely erroneous impression."

"Japan must work hand in hand with Great Britain—commercially and economically—now and in the future."

"Competition along commercial and economic lines is commendable," continued Mr. Nakano. "No treaty alliance can or should prevent or even curb this essential in the commercial life of a nation; but no Japanese business man can have

ill feeling toward Great Britain because
the British merchants have gained ground
in China while on the other hand, the
British commercial men in China should
not quarrel with us because we go there
as competitors. We are going elsewhere
as the trade competitors of our friends—
the British—and it is as you term it, 'a
square deal all round' But this business competition must not be allowed to
endanger the political relations of Great
Britain and Japan, which must remain intimate and friendly for all time to come.''

Baron Sakatani.

BARON SAKATANI ON A PERMA-NENT PEACE

Baron Sakatani, former Minister of Finance, Mayor of Tokyo, and the present delegate from Japan to the International Economic Conference to be held in Paris next month, is representative of a large school of thoughtful men among the leading Japanese gentlemen who have had touch with foreign affairs for the last decade.

Baron Sakatani graduated from the Imperial University with high honours in the year 1884 and soon afterwards entered the Department of Finance, where after successive promotions he held the Portfolio of Minister. He resigned as Minister of Finance in 1908 and then made a tour of the world. On his return, he was appointed Mayor of Tokyo, which post he occupied with distinction for three years.

In addition to his many official duties, Baron Sakatani has always taken a deep interest—active as well academic—in the leading members of The Japan Peace Society and in all his views and expressions has been extremely practical.

Baron Sakatani believes in the combination of Great Britain, Russia, France and the United States as the ideal alliance, by means of which a permanent and a lasting peace may be secured. It is a high ideal, but Baron Sakatani is not alone in his views which he has discussed with prominent statesmen and leaders of thought here in Japan, as well as abroad.

As is the case with the vast majority of the best of the Japanese men of standing and intelligence, Baron Sakatani has paid little attention to the tempest in a tea cup raised by the "Yamato" and a few student contributors, whose sophomoric contributions have been elaborately translated into a certain foreign newspaper for the purpose of creating an impression and building a foundation upon which to erect a "bogey."

Baron Sakatani said: "Among Japanese epigrams is that of the lover who says: 'I do not recollect you because I never forget you for so much as a single moment.'

"Who is there that for a moment can doubt the importance of the Anglo-Japanese Alliance to Japan and to England? I have not given the matter consideration because I have never for a moment doubted the effectiveness, the wisdom, or the permanence of this alliance.

"The Anglo-Japanese Alliance is of mutual importance, of mutual interest, and of mutual benefit. It is necessary. indeed, to the preservation of the world's peace.

"It is my ideal, nay—it is my firm conviction that the world's peace can be assured only in one way. The co-operation of the United States of America will complete a combination that would give us such assurance. If the United States of America will join with the allies and enter an agreement to assist Great Britain, France, Russia, and Japan in the maintenance of the peace, that peace which the world so longs for will be realized and ensured.

"Meanwhile, we will cling to the great alliance between Japan and Great Britain, believing it at this moment and for all time to come to be of vast importance and value."

The Hon. K. Minoura,
Minister of Communications.

VETERAN EDITOR AND CABINET MINISTER

"The criticisms of Great Britain and of the Anglo-Japanese Alliance do not constitute the voice of the people of Japan. They represent a very small voice of an extremely small class."

This is the opinion of the Hon. K. Minoura, Minister of Communications, one of the leaders of the Doshi-kai and veteran Editor-in-Chief of the "Hochi Shimbun," the newspaper reputed to have the largest circulation in Japan.

Few men among the leaders of thought in this country can lay stronger claim to attention than Mr. Minoura. He comes of the Samurai class and in himself has always represented the spirit of the Samurai. A graduate of Keio University, he commenced his newspaper career forty years ago. In 1878 he was appointed President of the Normal School at Sendai and in 1880 President of the Commercial School at Okayama. He has been a member of the House of Representatives since 1890 and for one session was Vice-President of the

House. Among the newspaper men of this country none stands higher or is held in greater respect. He was President of the National Press Association and President of the International Press Association for many years. As Editor-in-Chief of the "Hochi" he stood always with Count Okuma and at the present time may be regarded as voicing the popular side as the most thoroughly representative of the Commoners.

"I believe in the British Empire," Mr. Minoura went on, "I believe in what it stands for and I want to see a perfect understanding established and continued between the people of Great Britain and Japan.

"The utterances of opposition members in the Diet on matters of diplomacy are not based upon the furtherance of, nor do they signify, a definite policy. They are merely weapons with which to stir up feeling against, and attack, the Government. In these days of 'free speech' and 'free press' these discussions may go on in any country; though indeed in this case the time is not well chosen, and I sincerely hope that responsible persons will exercise greater care in the course of the discussion.

"But, while the utterances and the time selected are to be deplored, it must not be forgotten that some cause has been given for a feeling of impatience on the part of an element of the Japanese. ,, This comes from the continued reports of unfriendliness to Japan and to everything Japanese on the part of an element of the British residents and merchants in the Far East. Of course, I understand that this does not affect the real position of the two countries or the two peoples, and, of course, there may be two sides to the picture, but it seems a pity that the British residents in the Far East, who are generally of higher status than the merchant or shop-keeping class in England itself should allow prejudice, without reason, to sway their judgment and control their utterances. 'All I want to see is a greater breadth of view in the future.

"The detention of, and firing on, Japanese vessels by a British cruiser, unless really unavoidable, seem to me an unnecessary contribution to the resentments of a narrow class here and I sincerely hope greater care will be exercised.

"The present and the future call for perfect understanding between Great Britain and Japan. They must stand together for the ultimate peace of the world."

Mr. S. Shimada, President of The House of Representatives.

SPEAKER OF THE HOUSE

The Honourable Saburo Shimada was elected Speaker of Japan's House of Representatives because of a wide popularity and a reputation for strict honesty, coupled with frank and outspoken criticism of all things which he considered antagonistic to the interests of his country.

Mr. Shimada is a newspaper man, having been identified with the "Tokyo Mainichi" as President for many years. He visited the United States in 1910 and has a broad conception of the foreign relations of this country, having travelled throughout Europe in the years 1887 and 1888. Mr. Shimada is also an author, having written in the Japanese language "The History of the English Constitution," an essay on "The Revision of Treaties," and other important works.

"The newspaper reports emanating from China," said Mr. Shimada, "are calculated to estrange a certain sentiment in Japan from English sympathies. Correspondents and newspaper writers in that country have not been at pains to create the impression that the British community of China regarded the Japanese in a friendly light. Hence, there has come about a sense of uneasiness among a certain class of newspaper readers. But this in no way affects the Japanese public so far as the vast majority is concerned.

"The Japanese like the British people, and they uphold British ideals. The people of this country, as a whole, regard the Anglo-Japanese Alliance as a great factor in the future welfare of the country, as it has been of great benefit in the past. In times like this, however, too great care cannot be taken, and I most sincerely hope that our influential friends in Great Britain and British friends here will use every endeavour to clear up misunderstandings and direct the course of their own nationals in China in more kindly channels, while they may rest assured that we of Japan will in no way, nor at any time, falter in our fidelity to all our engagements and to all our friends.

"There is no disloyalty here, but there is a sensitiveness to superficial trifles that ought to receive the attention of the thinking classes."

H. E. Mr. Y. Ozaki, Minister of Justice.

MUST BE REAL AND ACVIVE

Minister of Justice in Characteristic Criticism Gives His Views on the Subject of the Alliance and Its Future Effectiveness

The Minister of Justice, Mr. Y. Ozaki, is one of the most widely known men in the Far East. He is known because of a fine independence of thought and speech, coupled with a high sense of patriotism and outspoken criticism, irrespective of party or personal influence, where he believes a criticism is called for, but at the same time a close guarding of the golden treasure of silence when speech is inadvisable. Mr. Ozaki has been a leading figure in the political life of Japan for the last fifteen years. He is a brilliant orator and at all times can command a large following among the masses of the people, as well as a respectful hearing in the Chambers of the Legislature. He has held a Cabinet place before and for many years held the responsible office of Mayor of Tokyo, which he resigned to re-enter the more active political field.

On the subject of the relations of Great Britain and Japan and the Anglo-Japanese Alliance, Mr. Ozaki said:

"It is needless to say that the Anglo-Japanese Alliance is indispensable both from the moral and political standpoints. Therefore, the Governments and statesmen of the two countries must always endeavour to protect the common interest and eliminate, as far as possible, causes of friction. There is no treaty alliance with respect to which the parties are entirely at one in every respect. In fact, if there were no points of difference there would be no need for alliances or agreements.

"But an alliance should not be left inactive and unchanging with changing conditions. Politicians and leaders of thought must at all times endeavour to maintain and keep the usefulness of the alliance abreast of the times. For this purpose, it is most essential that the authorities of the two countries keep in close touch and perfect understanding.

"The unfortunate incident of the Tenyo Maru and others could have been avoided if the authorities of England and Japan had previously reached a better understanding in regard to the policing of that part of the Eastern waters.

"And, not only the Government officials, but the people of the two nations must endeavour to maintain better understanding. For instance, there is a decided difference in the tone of the Press of England, and of this country in regard to China. The Press of Japan generally is anti-Yuan Shi-kai, whereas, the leading newspapers of Great Britain are favourably disposed to the Yuan regime. Such divergence of opinion between the peoples of the allied countries is regrettable. Here is an opportunity for thoughtful leaders of public opinion in both countries to bring about more complete unity of thought and consequently friendly relationship, based upon better understanding of an actual situation and not upon misconception and misinformation."

Mr. J. Inouye.

MR. J. INOUYE

The President of the Yokohama Specie Bank
Says it is an Important Guarantee of
Read Peace. The Influence of the
Bank of Japan as a Central
Government Institu-
tion &c.

Central Government Institution is extended to the smallest and most private
concern; but almost co-equal in its active
control and interwoven interests is the
Yokohama Specie Bank known all over
the world and every day becoming of
greater importance in its relations not only
to the banks of Japan but to the great
international houses of the world. Hence
the standing of the President of the Yokohama Specie Bank may be counted as
second to none. This important post was
in 1914 entrusted to Mr. J. Inouye, a
comparatively young man for so great a
trust and because of marked financial ability and tact, shown since that time through-

83

out the period of unprecedented difficulty, an appointment that has met with universal approval from those who know. Mr. Inouye is a graduate in Law from the Imperial University, but almost immediately he entered the service of the Bank of Japan, quickly rising to the position of Chief of Bureau. He then visited Europe and America and in 1911 was made Vice-President of the Yokohama Specie Bank. Discussing the position of Japan and the relations of this country and Great Britain Mr. Inouye said:—

"I have always been a staunch supporter of the Anglo-Japanese Alliance, and am strongly opposed to the stand taken by a section of our people in criticism of an agreement which, I consider, is the most important guarantee of peace in the Far East.

"It is true that competition exists in China between the merchants of the two countries and this clash of interested parties in China has caused a considerable amount of unfriendliness and criticism of the Anglo-Japanese Alliance on the part of the British residents in China, and unfortunately their views appear to be shared by some British people at home. These unfriendly criticisms have been communicated to this country, where a section of the Press took up the other side and thus the discussion began.

"I think this is most regrettable. Commercial competition is one thing and political co-operation is another. Despite trade rivalry, England and Japan are destined to stand together in their diplomatic activities. As long as the principle of equal opportunity is adhered to, and trade competition is fair the competition should not be allowed to interfere with the smooth working of a political alliance. Trade rivalry is nothing compared with the larger issues that are at stake. The Anglo-Japanese Alliance stands as the guarantee of peace and order in the Far East and of the integrity of China. If this guarantee is removed, there will be no end of trouble, resulting only in the destruction of trade and the vested interests of both Japan and England. This has been most clearly demonstrated in the present war. If Japan had not been here as the ally of Great Britain, British commercial interests would have suffered very materially.

"Therefore, commercial considerations must yield to the fundamental necessity of maintaining peace and order in the Orient. If one studies the situation a little deeper, it is clear that the commercial interests of neither country are suffering by reason of the Anglo-Japanese Alliance. Japan has established a sphere of

influence in Manchuria and Mongolia, and
England has asserted her superior position
in the Yangtze Valley. In both these
regions, the principle of the open door
and of equal opportunity must be maintained strictly. Both Great Britain and
Japan are prepared to uphold this principle in their respective spheres of influence. If this is so, there is left only
fair trade competition, which must continue even among merchants of the same
nationality.

"In discussing the future of the Anglo-
Japanese Alliance, the superior position
Japan now holds in the Far East must,
however, be taken into careful consideration. Japan has made great headway since
the alliance was first signed. Especially
since the commencement of the present
war, has Japan's position in the Far East
undergone a change. The part now played by Japan in the Orient is, I am sure,
fully appreciated by our ally, and due
recognition of it will be given when the
proper time arrives for the revision of the
treaty of alliance, although the present is
not the time to seek for or discuss any
changes."

Baron Megata.

BARON MEGATA ON JAPAN'S POSITION

Baron. Megata, for twenty-five years closely identified with the department of finance, later financial advisor to the Korean Government, prominent member of the House of Peers and active leader of the opposition is at the same time one of the ardent supporters of the Anglo-Japanese Alliance and friend of the people of the West. Baron Megata is in the very prime of active manhood, and since his graduation from the University of Harvard has been. recognized as one of the most progressive and, at the same time, most cautious and self-effacing of men. He said:

"The successful conclusion of the present war in Europe will bring into the fullest activity the usefulness of the Anglo-Japanese Alliance, which will continue to underlie all our international diplomatic policies.

"But it must not be allowed to work in a one-sided way, for in this lies the danger; nor must it be improperly used or construed. All agreements to be effective must be of mutual benefit and must work both ways. Any complaint that may be heard here in Japan is due to the manner in which certain of the terms of the Alliance have been carried into effect. These causes of complaint can be removed easily. Indeed, all the misunderstandings are of a quite minor character and do not really disturb relations or shake the foundation of the Alliance, though, if allowed to continue and if not checked by the application of the remedy to both sides, the trouble might become serious.

"The Anglo-Japanese Alliance stands for the peace of the Far East and for the maintenance of the integrity of China. We uphold these principles and as a demonstration of her absolute loyalty to her alliance and her friendship Japan declared war against Germany.

"England and Japan have by far the most predominant interests in the Far East and it is, therefore, the business of these two countries to maintain peace and secure the advancement and development of the Far East, so the governments and peoples, having the same beneficial objects in view, must work in accord and harmony. If interests and aims are one, a division of activity or diversity of opinion is waste and folly.

"Japan is the next-door neighbour of China, and Japan is the most deeply concerned in the maintenance of peace in the Orient. Therefore, because of this propinquity, geographically and economically, Japan must be prompt to assert her opinion, exert her influence and insist upon her rights in China in order to prevent waste by conflagration, breaches of the peace and illegal procedure. This should be the attitude of Japan, and I am quite sure that England will fully sympathise with our position.

"So long as this is done and clearly understood, so long as rights of position and sincerity of purpose are recognized by the people of the two nations, all will go well and there will be nothing to stay or to hinder the working of the Anglo-Japanese Alliance or the progress of good understanding between the two peoples. It should, however, be fully understood that no minor criticism or complaint or minor misunderstanding can shake the foundation of the Alliance."

Mr. Eikichi Kamada.

The President of Keio University, with its thousands of students, its tens of thousands of graduates, and its splendid history occupies a wonderfully advantageous position from which to collate and form opinions representative of a great mass of the really forceful and intellectual Japan. Mr. Eikichi Kamada, for the last thirty years, has been closely in touch with the educational system and institutions of this country. He has investigated the systems of Europe and America and has, in the author—"Education and Industry" and "Independence and Self-Respect." Mr. Kamada said:

"The alliance with Great Britain is a safeguard against disintegration and the course of a consistent career of usefulness, been honoured by being returned to the House of Representatives by the electorate of his native country and town of Wakayama. A man of great reserve force, his character is perhaps well illustrated in the titles of two books, of which he is the disease of unrest. Just as in a man's body some restraint and correcting influence is necessary to prevent disease and ensure healthy development, so with the national existence of Japan and of England. They can exist apart, but when upon them lies, as it does at present, the joint responsibility for the care of the Far East as a whole, they become as one and it is the alliance that keeps them together in healthy condition, but if the Alliance terms become one-sided the best influence of the specific is lost.

"At present, the Alliance terms appear to be one-sided, and, therefore, give opportunity for the criticism we have, unfortunately, heard recently. For instance, it would seem from the terms of the treaty that if England has trouble in India, Japan must send troops there; but if trouble should unhappily arise between America and Japan, England is not bound to assist Japan. For these reasons of the greater benefit derived by the greater party, an element of our people are not satisfied. Some even go so far as to say that the value of the Alliance has been lost to Japan. With this, however, I cannot agree. The Alliance is a safeguard and a guarantee of peace in the Far East and of co-operation in China, where there has always been danger of serious trouble. It is in China that England and Japan together hold the key.

"I want the Alliance continued, but when the proper time arrives I want to see it revised so as to ensure absolutely smooth working, entire absence of any note of dissatisfaction, and a sure guarantee of world's peace, if such a thing is possible, and, certainly, of peace in the Orient."

Vice-President Naruse.

BIG BANKER TALKS

Vice-President Naruse of the Nobles Bank Welcomes the Opportunity to Express His Views.

"The little outcry raised against our ally by a very small coterie of somewhat narrow vision, I am glad to notice has brought out a strong counter expression of real national sentiment loyal to Great Britain and sympathetic with our friends in their great struggle."

Vice-President Naruse, of the Fifteenth Bank, President of the Teiyu Bank, and connected with a number of important institutions, may be regarded as representative of the younger progressive financial element of Japan. After graduating from Keio University, Mr. Naruse went to America, where he took a post-graduate commercial course, and also in Law taking the degree of Batchelor and Master of Law at Cornell University in 1890. Since then, his work has all been in close connection with the leading financial institutions of this country.

Mr. Naruse has always maintained a close touch with the representative men of affairs of America, England and Europe, as well as with what may be regarded as the international institutions in Tokyo. He is always among the foremost in practical movements tending to create good relationship and understanding. The Tokyo Club, the Tokyo Lawn Tennis Club, the Tokyo Golf Club, the American University Club and kindred institutions that bring the East and West together in the close ties of good fellowship count Mr. Naruse among their strongest supporters and an ardent participator in their outdoor pastimes.

On the subject of Japan's relations with England and the attitude of the people of the country towards the people of Great Britain, Mr. Naruse was particularly emphatic and characteristically outspoken. He said:

"Recent mails from America have brought me newspapers and magazines containing reports that Japan is seriously considering the advisability of denouncing the Anglo-Japanese treaty of Alliance. I need hardly say that their reports come as a surprise and a shock to me. I suppose I may be considered sufficiently in touch with people and current events to be able to speak for an element of the representative men of Japan when I say

102

that among the bankers and financiers or among the well-informed, broad-minded people of this country no such thing is thought of and no such discussion is to be heard anywhere. The alleged anti-British sentiment literally does not exist, or, if it does, it is not among intelligent people.

"Those who may have argued against the Alliance must have done so in complete ignorance of the situation of this country, of Far-Eastern affairs and, indeed, in ignorance of what has been and is going on in the world outside. Such people must be unable to weigh properly the pros and the cons of this subject or to see things through large enough glasses.

"Of course, in any community, as in any club or household, there must be academic differences of opinion upon almost any subject that may arise, but while disputes may arouse a passing interest, arguments over the obvious do not receive much attention. So, perhaps, in this case, there may have been little debates over the Alliance, but if so they were along lines doubtless obvious; certainly at this time any discussion not only is useless, but it is in the worst taste. We do not care to consider for a passing moment now any possible future change of terms that may become obviously unavoidable and necessary in the days of reconstruction after the war.

"But if we should allow this discussion to go on and these reports to go out mis-representing Japan to the world, without a word on the other side, there might be real misunderstanding. Therefore, when I saw these false reports in foreign publications I thought it time for the representative men of Japan to speak out. I heartily welcome the opportunity offered by the 'Japan Times' and the Kokusai News Agency to join in the splendid and thoroughly representative' expression and concensus of opinion of the leading men of our country who unanimously stand for the Anglo-Japanese Alliance and who are always ready to demonstrate their friendship and sympathy for Great Britain—our ally."

Mr. Chujiro Matsuyama.

ASAHI'S EDITOR-IN-CHIEF

The Head of Japan's Morning Sun Says the Alliance is One of Japan's Quot Policies

The Editor-in-chief of the "Asahi Shimbun" of Tokyo occupies a splendid position in point of observation, influence and prestige in this country, as well as abroad. His views upon the subject of the relations between Great Britain and Japan, Englishmen and Japanese, as well as the Anglo-Japanese Alliance are, perhaps, of as high value to all concerned as those of any other man in public or private life.

"The "Asahi," or "Morning Sun" of Tokyo and of Osaka are newspapers of the highest standing in the Far East. In fact, no country can boast of a newspaper whose independence, enterprise and straightforward discussion of public questions have earned a more respectful hearing.

The "Asahi" stands for the best there is in the world's press and the members of its staff have qualified themselves for the positions they occupy.

Mr. Matsuyama has been for twenty years Editor of the "Asahi," either in Tokyo or Osaka, and, since 1901, has occupied his present position. He has also filled a number of responsible posts in the business and journalistic world.

In discussing this question, Mr. Matsuyama takes a stand in keeping with the reputation of his newspaper and for that reason his views will be received with the greater attention and consideration. Mr. Matsuyama said:

"It is a fact that among the Japanese there are some who question what benefit the Anglo-Japanese Alliance is giving to Japan. It is also a fact that some of them feel that Great Britain is monopolizing the benefit of the Alliance and Japan getting none.

"This is wrong, however, in my judgment. In order to maintain peace and promote advancement in the Far East, Japan must maintain the alliance with Great Britain and co-operate with Russia on land.

"Stating it more boldly, if Japan makes an enemy of Russia on land and of Great Britain on sea, she will be helpless in the Orient. Such a status may even threaten the foundation of the Empire. Japan being geographically isolated, we are more in need of the friendly alliance with Great Britain.

"I regret, however, tha' some of the

British in the Far East, especially those in China, show a tendency to dislike the Japanese. They charge that the Japanese encroach upon their sphere of activities but they do not seem to recognize the extent of the benefit they have derived because of Japan's friendship. They do not consider, for instance, how the British interests in the Orient might have been damaged if Japan had not declared war against Germany at the commencement of hostilities. They do not seem to appreciate what they must have lost in trade had the Germans not been held up in the Orient by Japan at a time when Great Britain alone was unable to handle even the one German ship "Emden," which was without base and a rover of the Far-Eastern seas. They do not remember that their commerce might have been stopped. They do not consider how they might have been greatly hampered in the despatch of Indian and Australian troops.

"The British subjects in China, without considering the benefits they have enjoyed because of Japan, seem to regard Japan and the Japanese simply as their political and commercial rivals—even enemies. We know, of course, that the British people at home do not agree with those in China, but some of the British officials and people in the Orient are not free from misunderstanding. I might be more personal in referring to Peking and Shanghai, but it is better not, perhaps. This unchara-

109

teristic British attitude I regard with the deepest regret. The recent talk among some element of Japanese in criticism of the Anglo-Japanese Alliance is chiefly due to these facts.

"But the Americans are also the competitors of the British in the Orient, so are the French, and the Germans were their keenest rivals before the war. The British merchant class, however, did not appear to view these through the same spectacles as the Japanese. This may tempt us to conclude that underneath, in the mind of the British people, there lies more or less racial prejudice.

"In Australia and in Canada no feeling was manifested against the French, the Americans, or even the Germans, but they were strongly opposed to the Japanese — their allies.

"However, in the great mass, Japan entertains only good will toward Great Britain and desires to perpetuate the Alliance. I only regret that certain British subjects in the Orient appear to hate Japan and the Japanese. Similarly, while the Japanese have the most friendly sentiment towards the American Government, many Japanese are liable to misunderstand America on account of the attitude of the Americans in California.

"The Anglo-Japanese Alliance, however, is absolutely necessary for both Great Britain and Japan. After the war,

110

Great Britain and Japan. After the war, Germany may attempt to regain her influence in the Orient with renewed vigor and may attempt to wreak vengeance especially on Japan. There may be others to possibly disturb the peace of the Orient, and so the Alliance is necessary in order to maintain tranquillity and to protect the interests of Great Britain and Japan.

"Those who doubt the value of the Alliance I would ask to imagine the situation were there no such alliance. They would find the absence of the Alliance a great inconvenience to the two countries. The intellectual British in the Orient will find the same thing, and the doubting Thomases on both sides—by trying to take a broad view—will understand more clearly.

"The Anglo-Japanese Alliance should be the basis of all diplomacy in the Far East."

Mr. Senkichiro Hayakawa.

JAPAN AND HER INCREASING CON-NECTIONS

A three or even four power pact and alliance is the theme of the statement made by Mr. Senkichiro Hayakawa, of the Mitsui Company, in discussing the relations between Great Britain and Japan.

Mr. Hayakawa, with a knowledge of the business man and interests of this country, takes a leading part, of course, in all developments of commerce and finance in his activities as the head of the great banking house of the Mitsuis. Mr. Hayakawa is a man of middle age in full vigor and with the broadest scope for his activities. His long connection with the financial side of the business necessarily has given him opportunity for the closest investigation, while his every-day touch with the business men of Japan must constitute him a high authority. He said:

"Japan owes a great debt of gratitude to Great Britain. We have always received a helping hand from that country on our way up the hill, for it has been a long, long slope we have had to climb

and are still climbing. Especially will
the assistance given to Japan by England
during the Russo-Japanese war never be
forgotten by us; therefore, because there
exists a trade rivalry in China or elsewhere, we are not going to take any position contrary to the letter or the spirit
of the Anglo-Japanese Alliance, nor can
we afford even the suggestion of such a
thing. We do not want to discuss the
Alliance now, except to say that it is a
great and a valuable treaty that will at
all times, in its broadest terms and spirit,
be observed by the Government and people of this country. This is no time for
petty criticisms or agitation along the lines
we have noted in some of the minor newspapers.

"The competition in trade is not of
such vast importance or magnitude as to
affect the fundamental policy of a nation.
Neither the merchants of Britain nor the
merchants of Japan are afraid of the competition of each other to any material extent. The competition can go on and increase as we all hope to go on and prosper
without in any way calling for a change
in the Alliance. No rule or healthy agreement can limit the activities of competition: The merchants of allied countries
will and, in fact, should compete.

"I know there are some who think that

the value of the Anglo-Japanese Alliance
has greatly diminished, but for my part,
I cannot see it. On the contrary, I firmly
believe the value of the Alliance has increased and is increasing.

"The new Russo-Japanese rapproach-
ment will add still greater strength to
the Anglo-Japanese Alliance. It is an addition to a great structure of defense
against future disturbance of smooth
commercial and political development.
The Russo-Japanese agreements now being
entered into are only another tower in
our fortifications and another guarantee
of peace.

"The wounds of the Manchurian campaign are healed, and now Russia and
Japan are on friendly terms. The present war has afforded us opportunity to
demonstrate our desire for friendship and
for peace. Russia is the ally fighting
shoulder to shoulder with Great Britain
in the present war, and so we have both
Great Britain and Russia as our active
allies.

"The time, therefore, has come for a
new triple alliance of Russia, Great Britain and Japan. In fact, a quadruple alliance may not be a dream, it may be a
natural outcome of the present position to
find France joined with us in the guarantee of amity and friendly tradal competition.

"In any case, I can say, without the
slightest hesitation or fear of contradic-

tion, that the value and the force of the
Anglo-Japanese Alliance is certainly tend:
ing to increase rather than decrease.''

Mr. K. Ishikawa,
Editor-in-Chief of the "Jiji."

MR. KANMEI ISHIKAWA

Mr. Kanmei Ishikawa, the Editor-in-Chief of the "Jiji," is regarded as one of the most able and well-balanced publicists in this country. He comes of the Samurai of Mito and, like the proprietor, as indeed all "Jiji" men, was educated at Keio. He has been at the head of the great newspaper since his graduation. Mr. Ishikawa has visited America, and Europe and is extremely broad in his views on international relations. Mr. Ishikawa said:

"The 'Jiji's' policy of recognizing the Anglo-Japanese Alliance as indispensable in assuring the integrity of China and the maintenance of peace in the Far East, as well as being the fundamental basis of Japanese diplomacy, is just the same to-day as it was yesterday and is not likely to change.

"Recently, there has been persistent talk about a Russo-Japanese Alliance. The relations between Japan and Russia have become far more close since the outbreak of the war, but we see no need to go fur ther and replace the existing understand ing with an alliance.

"If, after the war, a defensive alliance of Great Britain, Russia, France and the allies—with the Anglo-Japanese Alliance as its basis; is considered necessary we may be willing to join them. But, primarily we recognize the mutual benefit to be derived from the maintenance and perpetuation of the Anglo-Japanese Alliance."

The "Jiji," as a newspaper, stands for what is good in Japan. Founded by the great Yukichi Fukuzawa, the paper has been carried on by the family on a similarly high standard as "a gentleman's newspaper." It is among those of the larger newspapers of this country always to be found in the home and among the people who represent the real thought and intelligence of Japan. The present proprietor of the "Jiji," Mr. Sutejiro Fukuzawa is a journalist of the highest standing in this country. extremely popular among the employes of his newspapers here and in Osaka and especially proud of the standing and record of the "Jiji."

Mr. Fukuzawa was educated at Keio, of course, and afterwards at the Massachusetts Institute of Technology at Boston.

Dr. Juichi Soyeda.

DOCTOR JUICHI SOYEDA

"The need for the Anglo-Japanese Alliance is greater to-day than it was when the treaty was concluded and there is every evidence that the Alliance will become more and more firmly established as an essential guarantee of peace."

Doctor Juichi Soyeda, President of the Government Railways, former President of the Industrial Bank of Japan, special Finance Commissioner and among the best informed on all international affairs, speaks as one with high authority when he discusses the Anglo-Japanese Alliance and the relations between Britons and the people of this country. Doctor Soyeda is a graduate of the Imperial University, later taking post-graduate courses at Cambridge, England and Heidelberg, Germany. Since 1887, he has been closely connected with the financial affairs of this country. He has visited Europe and America several times on important missions and has a wide circle of close friends among leading men of the West.

After the above striking sentence, spoken

125

with careful emphasis, Doctor Soyeda continued:

"The Anglo-Japanese Alliance is not a piece of diplomatic opportunism. It has a high mission and it will fulfil that mission. It has as its ultimate purpose—the peace of the world. So long as there is any doubt as to that peace remaining permanent and beneficent, the Anglo-Japanese Alliance must stand. The longer it stands the better will be the understanding, and the closer the national friendship between Britons and Japanese. The Alliance is unassailable so long as there is this need for its continuance. It can never be broken by fractional strife, local political dissensions or temporary symptoms of unrest or impatience.

"Neither Great Britain nor Japan is responsible for the present rupture of the world's peace. But it is necessary that peace be secured as soon as it can be done in keeping with honor, dignity and safety. The co-operation of Japan and England makes for this peace. Great Britain now is taking the lead among the allies of Europe, while Japan is doing her best at this end in the fulfilment of the terms of the Alliance and in the pursuance of its object.

"Differences of opinion and divisions of sentiment are unavoidable, but these little straws are blown only by a fitful and uncertain breath of wind—an eddy here and there. They show nothing, indicate nothing, and mark no change in the fundamental opinion and temperament of this country or of our people.

"These minor questions—so easy to answer—must not be magnified into great problems. The thing that all men of Japan and of Great Britain must keep before them to-day is that the Anglo-Japanese Alliance is of vast significance and of tremendous importance, so great, indeed, that our enemies would be glad to see it broken. All the more reason, therefore, for us to say that it is of greater importance to-day than ever before and that its importance will increase—not decrease—as time goes by."

Mr. T. Tokonami,
Ex-President of Government Railways,
Leading Opposition Member of Diet.

VOICE FROM THE OPPOSITION

The entire unanimity of opinion in Japan with regard to the present war in Europe, Japanese friendship for Britishers and the Anglo-Japanese Alliance, does not change even when search is made among the leading commoners, members of Parliament and stalwart representatives of the Opposition to the present Cabinet. Under each of these three classes, the name of Mr. T. Tokonami, M.P., a member of the Seiyu-kai party, may be included with complete assurance. Mr. Tokonami has been identified with the activities of public life in Japan for the last fifteen years. Mr. Tokonami, though a young man, has held the most responsible positions, among them must be included Secretary to the Department of Finance, Vice-Minister of the Department of Home Affairs, President of the Railway Board and half a dozen other Government posts in the provinces. He is the President of the "Tokyo Maiyu" a daily newspaper representing the Opposition interests in politics which is of good standing. Mr. Tokonami, in an interview yesterday, said:

"I do not approve of the policy in diplomacy of the present Cabinet in many particulars, but the Anglo-Japanese Alliance is not a policy of this Cabinet and. in common with the whole people of Japan, I am in thorough sympathy with that Alliance.

"I cannot conceive a situation under which the people of Japan could be brought to denounce this Treaty of Alliance. We are not built that way and the suggestion that there is any thought of changing the terms or giving up the alliance at the present time is, in every way, contrary to the spirit of loyalty and chivalry of Japan.

"The so-called anti-British agitation represents but a very feeble minority. It is not supported by the intelligent class; neither is it likely to influence public opinion.

"Some of these light-headed agitators contend that the Anglo-Japanese Alliance is useless because Japan and Russia are now on friendly terms, but in my opinion our present cordial relations with Russia are based upon the Anglo-Japanese Alliance. In fact the rapprochement, in reality, results from the concert of England, Japan, Russia and France. England and Russia must stand together or fall together in the present war; they are in.

full agreement in every respect and therefore Japan must be willing to stand or fall
with her ally and friend and with the
friend of that friend. Hence, you will
see that it is because of England's friendship for Russia that the good relations of
Japan and Russia have reached the present point.

"Some people would have us believe that
Great Britain and Japan are at cross purposes in China. This is only an exaggerat-
ed and strained view to take of cases where
the private and individual interests of
Japanese and British merchants have
clashed. I do not for a moment believe
that the fundamental policies of the two
Governments conflict in China."

Mr. Nagahisa Uyeshima.

POPULAR NEWSPAPERS VIEWS

Nagahisa Uyeshima, for more than twenty years editor of the "Hochi Shimbun," has always been regarded as closely in touch with what has been called the great heart of the people. This, indeed, may always be said of the "Hochi" itself, for it is the newspaper of the people, as testified by the enormous circulation of both the Tokyo and Osaka editions. The foreigner coming to Japan and the people abroad are told many things about the "Hochi." Some of the stories are true. Anyhow, this newspaper has always been staunchly representative of the mass and in its utterances has at times earned the reputation of sensationalism. It also has the reputation of being controlled by Count Okuma and of being "anti" this or "anti" that. Doubtless, the liberality and extreme independence of official control, the admiration and loyalty of its proprietors and editors to Count Okuma and the extreme outspokenness of its editorial expression have given foundation for some of the assertions, though it may safely be stated that none of them is true.

Mr. Uyeshima is one of the early graduates of Waseda whose graduates are all loyal to Count. Okuma "the Sage of Waseda." Mr. Uyeshima is one of the most active of the organization known as the "Okuma Support Association." It is particularly interesting to place on record the views of this powerful representative of the newspaper world of Japan, and of one who can sway so great a mass of the people. Mr. Uyeshima said:

"The Anglo-Japanese Alliance is a guarantee of the world's peace. It was framed and signed as an answer to the popular demand in both countries. Great Britain controls extensive territory and large spheres of influence in Asia and in the South Seas. These she must protect and retain. Japan is also vitality interested in the maintenance of peace in the same territory because of her geographical position. She must at all cost safeguard them against intrusion by a disturbing element. So far, therefore, the interests of Japan and England are common and in perfect accord.

"Aside from this negative or defensive reason, Japan desires—by virtue of the Anglo-Japanese Alliance—to forward a

138

positive and constructive movement aiming at the destruction of race prejudice; harmonizing the civilization of the East and West, and realizing the ideal of universal brotherhood. England is broadminded and has little small racial hatred. Hence, fifteen years ago, when Japan was not what she is to-day, England entered into an alliance with Japan. We admire the broad-mindedness and wisdom of Great Britain, and hope to co-operate with her for all time to come.

"Also, behind our mutual interests and aspirations, there is the great moral and sympathetic tie of national characteristics. I always maintain that the English gentleman is a peaceful Samurai, and the Japanese Samurai is an armed gentleman. The basic ideals and the aspirations of the two are identically the same. Thus, the best of England and the best of Japan constitute a gentleman's brotherhood for East and West.

"The unity of political interests, moral aspirations and national ideals of Britain and Japan being then so apparent, it is regrettable to find some of our publicists airing imaginary grievances against our ally. But these outpourings are in reality the wails of the Opposition; they are more anti-Kasumigaseki than anti-British. Once these 'outs' hold the office and the

power they will immediately become pro-
British.   There are, it is true, certain
others among the scholars and intellectuals
who studied in Germany and are intoxi-
cated by the imaginary grandeur of the
German 'kultur' or by a spirit of admiration for 'force.' ↟ The extremists go
so far as to uphold the militaristic deli-
rium of Treitschke and almost unwitting-
ly find themselves in the German camp.

"But the German calculations and pre-
dictions have failed one after the other,
and these admirers of German ideals are
now being given a good object lesson.

"Another cause for the so-called anti-
British sentiment in this country is the
echo from voices raised by a section of
British residents in China against what
is alleged our Chinese policy. But our
actual Chinese policies have received the
endorsement of the British Government
and can, therefore, be regarded as the
common policy of England and Japan.
We place every confidence in the intelligence of Great Britain and believe that
the fact of the British policy in China
which, remaining unchanged and in harmony with Japan's, despite the criticisms
of her countrymen in China, will prove
to be an effective and wholesome remedy
for the inflamed minds of a section of our
own people.

"In conclusion, I wish to reiterate that both England and Japan disavow racial prejudice, regarding it as a slur upon their national reputation. Both England and Japan most emphatically repudiate the idea that one people, race, or nation can arrogate to themselves rights as 'superior:' or that they can conquer the rest of the world. These brothers of East and West are destined, sooner or later, to join hands in a fight for the common cause of universal justice.

"The people of Japan are fully cognizant of this fraternal relationship. They desire most amicable co-operation between Britain and Japan.

"The Japanese people compare the Anglo-Japanese Alliance with the Pacific Ocean. Sometimes the surface may be a little rough, but it always remains—pacific."

Mr. Robert P. Porter.

ROBERT P. PORTER

Mr. Robert P. Porter, of the staff of
"The Times" of London, was the guest of
honour yesterday at a luncheon given by
Doctor J. Soyeda. In the course of the
luncheon, Mr. Porter—responding to a
speech of welcome by Dr. Soyeda—made
special reference to the relations between
Great Britain and Japan. In view of the
great interest taken in this subject now and
the efforts made to bring about misunderstanding and ill will, the expression of
opinion from such a thoroughly-tried and
representative Englishman as Mr. Porter
is a splendid contribution, standing out as
it does in strong contrast to the views at-
tributed to Englishmen by writers in some
of the newspapers.

Mr. Porter may, perhaps, be said to be
one of the leading newspaper men and
correspondents in the active world of newspaper work to-day. A fine training in a
broad field and a mind of unusual capacity
in all matters of a business as well as a
diplomatic character constitute in **Mr.**
Porter a really high authority and it may
safely be said that his opinion, thus ex-

pressed, will carry great weight in clearing away the mist of doubt and suspicion which the enemies of Japan, England and Russia have reverently endeavoured to create.

Below are given Dr. Soyeda's speech of welcome and Mr. Porter's response:—

Dr. Soyeda's Speech

"The London 'Times' needs no introduction and therefore Mr. Porter's arrival here with the special object of introducing Japan to the world through the influential paper which he represents, must be received with the heartiest welcome.

"It appears to me that the world does not understand our country properly, and though I am confident that the part which Japan has undertaken in the interest of the Allies since the outbreak of this calamitous war must have received due appreciation, I fear it may take some time before Japan's real intention and position are fully recognized by the world.

"To our greatest regret we find now and then that the attitude of Japan is viewed with suspicion, this suspicion being entirely traceable to misunderstandings. Such misunderstandings must be speedily cleared up, especially between the two Island Empires so closely allied. The two Powers, one in the West, and the other in the East, are bound by solemn compact to maintain by joint effort the peace of the world, and they can hardly fulfil this grave mission unless they regard each other with trust and respect. Their union and co-operation is necessary, not merely for the sake of the two Powers, but for the sake of peace and humanity.

"Viewed in this way Mr. Porter's visit must be regarded as opportune as it is of grave significance, and every facility, therefore, must be extended to him to make his mission a success.

"We trust he will spare no efforts for the work he has in view, as we are sure he will render thereby boundless good, not only to the public of the two allied nations, but towards ultimately furthering the cause of peace and humanity."

Mr. Porter's Response

"I wish to thank you on behalf of my paper for the cordial welcome you have given me, and for the generous reference to 'The Times.' Dr. Soyeda and many present here are no strangers to me, and on my two former visits to your fascinating country I have been the recipient of your generous hospitality and assistance.

"I am fully in accord with my friend, Dr. Soyeda, when he says that he is confident that the part taken by Japan in the great war has received due appreciation throughout the length and breadth of my

native land. The splendid work Japan did
at Tsingtao is appreciated and there is
not a Briton who does not say 'you did
your bit well' and 'made a clean job of
it.' The intervention of Japan in the
war, as you know, was made in response to
a direct request from Britain and not from
any desire on the part of Japan. For your
work at Tsingtao you won British gratitude. Japan long ago won British admiration. .Whatever may be true in respect to
other countries, I have never heard Japan's
real intentions and position viewed with
suspicion in the United Kingdom. British
statesmanship, as I have said, openly and
straightforwardly asked you to enter the
war side by side with British troops. It
was full partnership with no reservations.
one of mutual trust and respect. What-
ever kinds there may be in John Bull's
character, fickleness is not one of them. To
him the Anglo-Japanese Alliance is as Dr.
Soyeda says 'a solemn compact.'

"The present is, therefore, no time for
crude generalizations on the relations of
the two great Island Empires, but for the
exercise of patience and tenacity and the
qualities of true greatness which the Japanese displayed on the splendidly fought bat-
tlefields of Manchuria. Japan and Great
Britain are allies in a world-wide war in
which Great Britain is pouring forth her

blood and wealth in a manner almost inconceivable to those who have not lived there and seen for themselves the splendid efforts your great ally is making.

"If there exist misunderstandings , by all means clear them away, but from my point of view, I confess I see no misuncerstandings between the two Island empires which are so closely allied, except such as may arise from the suspicions engendered by the enemies of both nations and those more or less traceable to the same perfidious source which during the war has increasingly endeavoured to create misunderstanding between America and England.

"In conclusion, let me assure you that all that possibly can be done has been done to aid me. No effort has been spared on your part to help or to give me facilities for obtaining information firsthand. For this assistance permit me to take this opportunity to thank not only those present but many others who have taken a practica interest in my work. If my mission should not prove successful, you gentlemen will be held blameless, excepting in so far as your generous hospitality may undermine my activities and reduce the output of copy."

大正五年五月二十五日印刷
大正五年五月二十九日發行

著作權所有

金拾錢

編纂者　東京市麴町區内幸町一丁目五番地
國際通信社
代表者
ジェー、アール、ケネデー

發行者　東京市麴町區内幸町一丁目五番地
ジャパン、タイムス社
代表者
ジェー、アール、ケネデー

印刷者　東京府豊多摩郡淀橋町角筈八百五十六番地
高橋勝雄

印刷所　東京市麴町區内幸町一丁目五番地
ジャパン、タイムス社印刷部